Series / Number 90-019

Catholicism and the Franco Regime

NORMAN B. COOPER

University of Reading

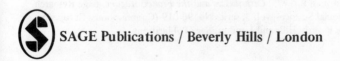

SAGE Publications / Beverly Hills / London

For information address:

SAGE Publications, Inc.
275 South Beverly Drive
Beverly Hills, California 90212

SAGE Publications, Ltd.
St George's House / 44 Hatton Garden
London EC1N 8ER

International Standard Book Number 0-8039-9938-0

Library of Congress Catalog Card No. L.C.-74-21382

FIRST PRINTING

When citing a Research Paper, please use the proper form. Remember to cite the series title and include the paper number. One of the two following formats can be adapted (depending on the style manual used):

(1) COOPER, N. (1975) "Catholicism and the Franco Regime." Sage Research Papers in the Social Sciences (Contemporary European Studies Series, No. 90-019). Beverly Hills and London: Sage Publications.

OR

(2) Cooper, Norman B. 1975. *Catholicism and the Franco Regime.* Sage Research Papers in the Social Sciences, vol. 3, series No. 90-019 (Contemporary European Studies Series). Beverly Hills and London: Sage Publications.

Contents

NORMAN COOPER graduated in Spanish at the University of Birmingham. He has done post-graduate work at the Universities of Bristol, Wales, Reading, and Salamanca, and has taught English in Madrid and Spanish in London. He holds an M.A. from Reading, where he was recently seconded to the University Graduate School, working with Professor Hugh Thomas and Mr. Paul Preston.

CATHOLICISM AND THE FRANCO REGIME

NORMAN B. COOPER

University of Reading

INTRODUCTION

Human organizations tend to adapt to situations to ensure survival; the Spanish Catholic Church is no exception. It has long been regarded as the most rigid and uncompromising in Europe, but it has within it elements which enable it to adjust to prevailing circumstances. In the nineteenth century it adopted an ultramontane position supporting Carlism in its struggle against emergent liberal Capitalism. However, with the latter's inevitable ascendancy, it changed course throwing in its lot with the new bourgeois order. It became reconciled to the *desamortización* policy whereby its lands were largely confiscated by successive governments and sold off to the *nouveau riche*. By the end of the century the Church, though still denouncing liberalism as a fundamental heresy, was rapidly becoming integrated into the liberal capitalist world. With the increasing political awareness of the working classes in the early part of the twentieth century, an alliance was forged between the new bourgeoisie and the old land-owning oligarchy and the Church identified itself with these power groups. It enjoyed a privileged position during the Restoration period and the dictatorship of Primo de Rivera. Those in power wished the Church to continue its traditional function with regard to the maintenance of social order and, with virtually complete control over education, the Church was only too willing to comply. However, within the middle classes there still remained anti-clerical liberals whose aim it was to Europeanize Spain and to curb the influence of the Church. This intellectual elite were to become the spokesmen of the reforming spirit of the Second Republic of April 1931. The attempt by the Republic to create a secular Constitution including drastic curtailment of the Church's influence, especially in the field of education, inevitably increased the Church's militancy, and it is hardly surprising that when the Civil War erupted in July 1936, clerical support

AUTHOR'S NOTE: Since the completion of this essay a full length study of the ACNP has been published: A. Saez Alba, La otra Cosa Nostra (Paris, Ruedo Iberico 1974).

5

was overwhelmingly in favour of the military rebellion. With the victory of the insurgents, the Church was granted an almost unparalleled pre-eminence in the new State. But cordial relations between Church and State under Franco were to change radically as the Church felt the necessity once again to adapt itself to new circumstances in the late 1960s. The last forty years have seen a striking transformation in Church/State relations and in the role of Catholicism in Spain. The position today remains uneasy and the future uncertain.

THE CRUSADE
THE CHURCH AND THE MILITARY RISING

Franco's *pronunciamiento* issued on 18 July in Las Palmas makes ironic reading.[1] It makes no mention whatsoever of religion. Franco's personal indifference to Catholicism during his youth is well-known, and perhaps not very significant. However, the lack of even a brief word on the subject in the manifesto is extremely revealing. The future caudillo shows himself extremely concerned that 'los monumentos y tesoros artísticos son objeto de los más enconados ataques de las hordas revolucionarias' but does not refer to the burning of churches. He is concerned for the Constitution (sic), the Judiciary, the Army, but apparently not the Church. Most ironic of all is his final invocation of 'la trilogía fraternidad libertad e igualdad' – 'por este orden' he adds, very significantly. So the saviour of Spain's intransigent Church concludes his statement by calling on the basic tenets of the French Revolution, against which the Church had been fighting a bitter struggle for over a century. After his statement the General busied himself with how he would obtain the help of the 'pagan' Hitler to transport the mostly Moslem Army of Africa across to Spain from Morocco. The crusade's origins were indeed extraordinary as regards the attitude of its future leader.

In Spain itself things were rather different. The clergy in the rebel areas – with one crucial exception – greeted the rising with relief, though General Mola was also dilatory in adopting the jargon of the 'cruzada'.[2] The hierarchy were to be seen giving their open support for the rising, blessing falangist militia and appearing in public ceremonies with the generals, even when the declared intention of many of the latter was to 'save the Republic'. The famous photograph of clerics giving the fascist salute is remarkable because most of the insurgent officers photographed are not doing so.[3] Antonio Bahamonde and Ruiz Vilaplana. in their classic primary accounts of life in rebel Spain,

6

describe graphically the part played by the clergy in the early days of the war[4] especially the key role of Cardinal Ilundaín in Seville. As for 'Franco Africanus', he seems to have been unaware at first of the tremendous importance Church support was to mean for him. However, he soon adapted his attitude and vocabulary to meet the new situation in accordance with his role as crusader.[5]

THE IMPORTANCE OF THE HIERARCHY

The majority of Spanish bishops had been bitterly hostile to the Republic. Cardinal Segura's diatribe on 7 May 1931, in which he urged Catholics to oppose the Republic, set the tone for clerical antagonism. The debate over Article 26 of the Republican Constitution and the subsequent *Ley de Confesiones y Congregaciones* polarized Spain on the issue of the relations between Church and State, particularly with regard to education, civil marriage, divorce and the position of the Regular Orders. The Spanish Church was the most backward-looking in Europe, and largely supported the 'Integrist' position as against the 'Modernist' school of thought. The term 'Integrism' needs careful definition in the Spanish context. It must be defined in two ways, related but distinct. 'Integrismo' in its narrower sense represents the extreme wing of the Carlist movement, epitomized by Cándido Nocedal and his son Ramón Nocedal Romea, who led the reaction against the alleged 'progressive' tendencies which they saw contaminating the views of the Carlist royal family itself. However, 'Integrism' in its broader sense was a movement which was found all over Catholic Europe, and was opposed to the 'Modernist' attitude which was beginning to permeate the Church during the late 19th and early 20th centuries. The Integrist position was set out most clearly in the Encyclical *Pascendi Gregis* of Pope Pius X, issued in 1907 'on the Doctrines of the Modernists'. This encyclical was much influenced in its view by the attitudes of Cardinals Billot and Benigni (later to be supporters of *Action Française* and Italian Fascism respectively) and that of Cardinal Merry del Val, Pius X's Secretary of State and a member of a well-known family in the Spanish oligarchy. The Integrists demanded complete clerical domination of education and censorship, condemned freedom of worship and insisted on the 'integrity' i.e. *totality* of Catholic dogma, re-affirming belief in the doctrines of Pope Pius IX, and the *Syllabus Errorum* of 1864. It was in defence of this form of Catholicism that the Spanish Church backed the 1936 rising. So in this sense *all* Carlists were 'integrists', as well as the majority of militant Catholics in other groups including virtually the entire hierarchy. They were fighting rationalism, socialism, communism, laicism, liberalism and, perhaps above all, Freemasonry. The fact that many of the rebel officers were themselves Masons is noteworthy; their motives were, more overtly, the defence of order and privilege. Leader of the hierarchy was Segura's successor Cardinal Isidro Gomá y Tomás. He was in Carlist Pamplona on 18 July 1936. The significance of this fact has led to much speculation. Whatever his motives for being there, he refrained from throwing his enormous influence behind the rising until rebel successes had indicated that a favourable outcome could be anticipated. He then broadcast his famous message to the defenders of the Alcázar on 28 September 1936. The ferocity of his language was remarkable. He spoke of the 'alma bastarda de hijos de Moscú . . . y con ellos van los judíos y los masones . . . las sociedades tenebrosas manejadas por el internacionalismo semita'.[6] Cardinal Ilundaín and Archbishop García Castro of Burgos were also particularly prominent. and lesser dignitaries followed their lead. Bishop Luciano Pérez Platero of Segovia issued a pastoral on 20 September — before Gomá's broadcast — stating that the rising was 'cien veces mas importante que la reconquista' because its effects would be more permanent.[7] Bishop Plá y Deniel of Salamanca was inevitably brought into close contact with the leaders of the rising. His main contribution at this time was a pastoral published on the same day as Gomá's broadcast, inspired by the relief of the Alcázar. It was called *Las dos ciudades* and was based upon the Agustinian image of the Cities of God and of the Devil; the victorious counter-revolution (the term is used quite frankly) is likened to the City of God, triumphant over Communism and Anarchism, the children of Cain.[8] Moreover the lay organization Catholic Action, firmly controlled at that time by the hierarchy, had declared itself 'enthusiastically' for the rising at its Congress in Burgos in September 1936.[9]

Cardinal Gomá followed up his broadcast with a pamphlet *El caso de España* explaining his justification for the rising, but the greatest service he did for Franco was of course the collective letter 'To the Bishops of the Whole World' published on 1 July 1937, signed by two Cardinals (Gomá and Ilundaín — Segura being still in exile) six Archbishops, thirty-five Bishops and five Vicars-General. The Bishop of Orihuela was ill, and according to Thomas his vicar-general, Mgr. Ponce, signed on his behalf, though this is denied by Tuñón de Lara.[10] Far more significant was the absence of the signatures of Cardinal Vidal y Barraquer of Tarragona, interim primate of Spain before Gomá's nomination, and Bishop Mateo Mugica of Vitoria. Cardinal Vidal was perhaps the only 'liberal' in the hierarchy at that time and had tried

under the Republic to improve relations with the government.[11]
Mugica's case is discussed below. The Collective Letter was clearly
written in an attempt to allay the doubts of foreign Catholics regarding
the legitimacy of the 'Cruzada'. Franco apparently requested Gomá to
obtain such a written statement regarding the hierarchy's support for
the rising.[12] The letter was written by Gomá on 15 May and sent for
signature on 7 June. Its contents are well-known. It speaks of an
'armed plebiscite' against the enemies of religion, speaks of the 'foreign
influence' which had deceived the Spanish people and rejoiced that the
vast majority of the 'communists' had become reconciled to the Church
before death, a gruesome touch for the modern reader. It also insisted
on the 'documentary proof' regarding a 'communist plot' which the
rebels had forestalled. The letter convinced many foreign Catholics and
for many in Europe it was unnecessary and belated. In fact the German
bishops had issued a collective pastoral at Fulda as early as 19 August
1936. This backed Hitler's support for Franco. It looked forward to a
Europe 'cleansed from Bolshevism' with the words 'May our Führer,
with God's help, succeed in completing this terribly difficult undertaking
with an unshakeable determination and faithful participation of all
Volksgenossen'.[13] Only one week earlier the Reich Propaganda Ministry
had denied intervention.[14] However, many Catholic intellectuals,
particularly in France, were unimpressed.

The bishops' example was followed by the Spanish clergy. Support
for the crusade was to be expected from the fanatical chaplains of the
requetés, but even the Falange took on an odour of sanctity. The
Falangist priest, Fr. Fermín Yzurdiaga became Franco's Press and Propaganda chief at Salamanca, against the wishes of Gomá[15] — priests are
forbidden such posts by the encyclical *Pacendi Gregis*. The secular
clergy railed from their pulpits against the 'reds'. The Jesuits — who had
been most affected by Republican legislation — had efficient propagandists for Franco in Fr. Menéndez Reigada (*La Guerra Nacional
Española ante la Moral y el Derecho*) and Fr. Constantino Bayle (*¿ Que
pasa en España?*) who both published important polemics in Salamanca
in 1937. Yzurdiaga gave the crusader-falangist view in his *Discurso al
silencio y voz de la Falange*. In spite of all this support there remained a
disquieting element for the rebels — the attitude of the Basques.

THE BASQUE CATHOLICS

The Basques were a problem for the insurgents. The term 'rojos'
hardly suited them. Traditionally the most truly pious of all Spanish

Catholics, they largely remained implacable enemies of Franco, and the crusade myth was clearly belied by their struggle. Of course many Basques assisted the rebels; the Civil War was truly fratricidal. The Requetés and the defenders of Bilbao were historically closely linked. It was on the Basques that the insurgents' fury was unleashed following the rebels' failure to take Madrid.

Already in early August Cardinal Gomá had tried to persuade the bishops of Pamplona and Vitoria to sign a pastoral supporting the rising in spite of the fact that the Cardinal Primate himself had not yet spoken out clearly. The pastoral was *broadcast* on 6 August before the Bishop of Vitoria had in fact signed it.[16]

A most pathetic figure in the Spanish struggle is Bishop Mgr. Mateo Mugica. A monarchist and friend of Segura, his attitude to the rising remained ambiguous. His failure to condone the rising soon made him persona non grata and he was sent to Rome by Cardinal Gomá and urged to keep silent regarding his reservations. In October fourteen Basque priests were executed by firing squad by the insurgents. When the news leaked out the disturbance caused in foreign Catholic circles was considerable. According to Canon Law, Catholics who perpetrate such an act are automatically excommunicate. Gomá wrote an open letter to President Aguirre stating that he had intervened with the rebels to urge them not to repeat such actions although he did not condemn the executions as such. The position in Canon Law of the entire rebel and pro-rebel leadership, from Franco and Gomá downwards, with regard to these shootings has never been clarified.[17]

French Catholic intellectuals prepared a petition in February 1937 calling for an end to the war, and placing the responsibility for it on the Francoists. It was signed by Jacques Maritain and many others but not by Francois Mauriac, who did, however, sign a further manifesto in May 1937 following the bombardments of Guernica and Durango. Maritain and Bidault were among the signatories. This anti-Franco Catholic activity in France inspired Cardinal Pacelli to issue a statement requesting that Gomá again intervene with Franco to urge more moderation in military activities in Vizcaya.[18]

THE ATTITUDE OF THE VATICAN

Papal involvement with fascism has been a controversial issue for fifty years. With regard to the Spanish conflict the tone was set for anti-democratic activity by Catholics by the Encyclical *Quadragesimo Anno* of Pius XI published in 1931 four weeks after the declaration of the Republic and one week after Cardinal Segura's notorious pastoral. The encyclical was concerned with 'the social order' and celebrates the fortieth anniversary of *Rerum Novarum* of Leo XIII, the most important statement hitherto issued regarding the Papal attitude to socio-political affairs. *Quadragesimo Anno* is a carefully worded document, with much space devoted to 'social justice', the 'just wage' etc. but stressing the right to property and repeating the condemnation of liberalism and socialism, stating (Clause 120) that 'Catholic and Socialist are contradictory terms'. It calls for 'soldiers of Christ to oppose the havoc which could befall mankind', (Clause 144) and, most ominously, contains praise for the corporate state, based upon vertical syndicates and the abolition of strikes (Clauses 91–5).[19] In June 1933 there followed *Dilectissima Nobis* which attacked laicism and supported the Spanish hierarchy's struggle against the Republican constitution.[20] Following the outbreak of war Pius XI addressed 500 Spanish refugees at Castelgandolfo on 14 September 1936. The Pope was guarded in his choice of words and mentioned no names. However, his support for the rising was very thinly veiled, and he directed his blessing on those who 'had taken on the task of defending God and religion'.[21] Official approval followed one year later, when the Vatican recognized the Franco government. Recognition was preceded by further encyclicals. The famous *Divini Redemptoris* of 19 March 1937 summarized the Church's attitude to Communism, and contained a chapter on 'Communist Horrors in Spain' and came out openly on the side of those fighting in Spain to prevent the spread of Marxism. *Firmissimam Constantium* of 28 March, though specifically aimed at Mexico, was also important. It upheld the right of Catholics to take up arms against hostile governments. Pius XI was 80 years old, and it is not difficult to detect the hand of Pacelli in these Papal statements. However, the Cardinal Secretary of State was unsuccessful when he attempted to persuade the aged Pope to include the collective letter of the Spanish bishops in the Vatican *Acta Apostolica Sedis.*[22] On 7 October 1937 Franco received the Papal Apostolic Delegate Mgr. Ildebrando Antoniutti, subsequently to become a cardinal and a leading member of the reactionary element in the Roman curia. He was to be one of the leading propagandists of the 'Cruzada' later when he returned as Nuncio to remain for nine years before his elevation to the curia.[23] Meanwhile the first full Nuncio to Franco, Mgr. Gaetano Cicognani, presented credentials on 24 June 1938, and José Yanguas Messía did likewise at Rome. The Vatican link with Franco was completely forged at last.

THE VICTORY

*Lifting up our heart to God we give sincere thanks with your
Excellency for Spain's Catholic victory.*

Thus read a telegram of congratulation received by General
Francisco Franco on 31 March 1939 following the successful conclusion
of his rebellion against the Spanish Second Republic.[24] The sender of
this telegram was the newly-enthroned Pope Pius XII.

On 16 April 1939 the Pope followed this message with a more
extended statement in Spanish read over Vatican Radio.[25] This
discourse, known as 'Con inmenso gozo', eulogizes the victory achieved
by the Christian heroism of the Spanish defenders of religion. He
alludes to the words spoken by his predecessor, Pius XI, to Spanish
refugees on 14 September 1936[26] and says that the papal blessing given
that day contributed to the providential outcome of the War. He speaks
of Spain 'bulwark of the faith' and of Franco whose 'noble and Christian
sentiments' would be the guarantee of future justice. He goes on to say
that the duty of the victors in their task of 'pacification' should be
carried out in accordance with the principles of the Church, and
expresses the hope that the defeated 'deceived by materialism' should
return like the prodigal son to the paternal house. He pays tribute to
those who died 'for their faith in Jesus Christ'. Regarding the Basques
and other Catholics who died for the Republic, he naturally remains
silent. He ends his statement with his blessing on the chief of state, the
government and 'all children of Catholic Spain'.

The victory of 1939 was shared between the Church and the
Totalitarian Fascist State. This was an uneasy alliance. 'Statism' was
opposed by the Church and the attempts by Franco's allies Mussolini and
Hitler to subordinate Church privileges, especially in education, to the
State had aroused the irritation of the Vatican, and produced two
encyclicals from Pius XI *Non abbiamo bisogno* (1931) and *Mit
brennender Sorge* in 1937, publication of the latter in Spain having
been suppressed by Franco and the primate Cardinal Gomá y Tomás.
However, the new Falange of April 1937 had been largely purged of
anticlerical elements, and the way was clear for the restoration of
Church dominance in Spanish life. Fernández Cuesta stressed Falange
allegiance to the Church at the first postwar Consejo Nacional de FET
y de las JONS in June 1939.[27] The laic legislation of the Republic was
revoked as was freedom of religious worship. The regular orders were
allowed to return in force and the clerical grip on education was
allowed to become greater than for a hundred years. Catholic

observance and instruction became compulsory in all schools. The *Nuevo Ripalda* integrist catechism was restored and it was once more taught that the reading of liberal newspapers (apart from the Stock Exchange page) was mortal sin.[28] There were, of course, no liberal newspapers to be read, since a major concession was made by Franco to the Church in the field of censorship of communication media. Even *El Debate* fell by the wayside. Only Church publications were exempt from censorship, a fact which was to bring about serious trouble for the regime many years later. The 1943 University Law stated that university instruction should be adapted to Catholic dogma.

The gaols, full of political prisoners, were invaded by chaplains eager to convert the impenitent liberals, marxists and anarchists. The chaplains also were given another great opportunity for proselytization in the barracks with the introduction of compulsory military service. The 'rechristianization' of Spain was their lofty aim.

In return Franco's 'cruzada' was sanctified by the Church, the myth of José Antonio took on a religiose aura and Spain was held up as a model of Christian civilization. Franco, however, was much concerned with practical matters. He came to an agreement with the Vatican on 7 June 1941 renewing for himself the traditional right of patronage of the Spanish monarchs regarding the nomination of bishops. Franco thus retained the right of final choice in any permanent appointment to a residential see. This was a crucial means of ensuring loyalty among the hierarchy.

THE ROLE OF CATHOLIC ACTION

The Falange had been exultant in the summer of 1939. They hoped that at last their imperialist daydreams would be realized, as the new Europe of Axis totalitarianism would restore to Spain her rightful claims. However, as time went on, and Franco refused to be wooed into another total war, they became uneasy. Thousands went to Russia to fight and die, in continuation of the crusade against Bolshevism. But 'Operation Felix', which was to recover Gibraltar with Hitler's help, never materialized, and the allied landing in North Africa — on Spanish territory according to the Falange — went uncontested by Spaniards. Clearly, Falangist imperialism was already beginning to look absurd. Franco was to stake his survival on Catholicism, an ideology rather older than Falangism, and likely to stay the course longer. The Church hierarchy were with him, and they had under their control over 300,000 members of Acción Católica Española, an organization which gradually assumed ever more importance in Spain.[29] Pius X and Pius XI had encouraged Catholic Action to become the organization by which the Church was to galvanise the laity against the dangers of Marxism. The absolute authority of the hierarchy was stressed. In Spain the *Junta Suprema* was identical with the Conference of Bishops under the Pontifical Directorate of the Primate. The *Dirección Central* consisted of five bishops with the crucial addition of one layman, who served as director of the lay organization the *Junta Técnica* or *Junta Central.*

The first Congress of ACE was held in 1929 under Cardinal Segura. The political wing of Catholic Action was to become Acción Popular and its intellectual focus the newspaper *El Debate* under Ángel Herrera Oria, and much influenced by the then nuncio Mgr. Tedeschini. Their policy was that however much they might deplore the passing of the monarchy, it was the duty of the faithful to work for Catholic principles under whatever regime they found themselves. The encyclical *Quadragesimo Anno* of 1931, with its 'social' yet antidemocratic tone inclined many of the group towards a corporatist solution of the class warfare that they believed to be destroying Spain.

Closely linked with Catholic Action was the elitist pressure group ACNP (*Asociación Católica Nacional de Propagandistas*) founded in 1909 by the Jesuit Fr. Ángel Ayala as a reaction against the allegedly anticlerical policies of Prime Minister Canalejas. This was an extension of the *Congregaciones Marianas* or 'Luises' the former pupils' associations of Jesuit schools. The ACNP soon came to dominate Catholic Action under the leadership of Herrera. Unlike ACE itself, the ACNP was a lay organization not linked officially to the hierarchy. It thus had correspondingly greater freedom of movement in the political sphere. The 'propagandistas' were prominent not only in the CEDA but in the PNV, Aguirre himself being a member.

The CEDA defeat in February 1936 disillusioned many ACNP members, and Herrera himself resigned from its leadership. He was succeeded by Fernando Martín-Sánchez Juliá. Herrera was soon to embark upon his clerical career, which was to lead him to the rank of Cardinal.

Franco found an army of enthusiastic helpers among the ranks of Catholic Action, the ACNP and the 'Luises'.[30] The latter staged vast demonstrations in his favour, and much reference was made to the blood of the 7,000 martyrs, members of Catholic Action who had died on the insurgent side. *Ya* became a flourishing daily newspaper run by *Editorial Católica* under the editorship of Fr. Pedro Cantero, later to become Archbishop of Zaragoza, who summed up the attitude of Catholic Action and its associated groups in an editorial in September

1942 entitled *Al lado de Franco*.[31]

Membership of Catholic Action was by no means incompatible with Falangism. The co-author of the rabidly falangist *Revindicaciones de España*, Fernando María de Castiella, decorated by Hitler for gallantry,[32] was simultaneously head of the Falange's *Instituto de Estudios Políticos* and active in the ACNP.

Alberto Martín Artajo was president of the Junta Técnica of ACE during the war years. A graduate of the Jesuit Deusto University and therefore prominent in the *Congregaciones Marianas*, he had served Franco well since 1938, when he undertook a tour of foreign Catholic universities lecturing on the validity of the 'Cruzada'. He was a close friend of the new primate, Cardinal Plá, former Bishop of Salamanca during the days of the Cuartel General. The caudillo decided to appoint Martín Artajo foreign minister in 1945, thereby attempting to put on a brave front vis-à-vis the victorious European democracies. The Church had seen the writing on the wall for the Axis, and were now condemning 'totalitarianism' — Cardinal Plá succeeded in September 1945 in condemning totalitarianism and praising Franco in the same pastoral letter.[33] Some clergy were unrepentantly profascist. The Bishop of Madrid-Alcalá Mgr. Eijó y Garay had forbidden the sacraments to those French citizens resident in Madrid who were not loyal to Vichy.[34] The 'Blue Bishop' was to prove an embarrassment to Franco's foreign propaganda for nearly twenty more years.

The Axis defeat brought with it Franco's isolation, and Martín Artajo became foreign minister at a very difficult time. Franco hoped to impress European Christian Democrat parties, and a new Concordat with the Vatican was the best means of ensuring his respectability.

NEGOTIATIONS FOR THE CONCORDAT

Martín Artajo as foreign minister was to be assisted in negotiations with the Vatican by his ACNP colleague Joaquín Ruíz Giménez, appointed as ambassador to the Holy See in 1948. These men had another important link; they were both prominent in *Pax Romana*, the international Catholic university organization founded in 1921. In every way they justified Franco's faith in them, for the Concordat was a triumph.

It was long in coming, however. The hostility of the victorious powers towards Franco made Pius XII wary. There was talk that Franco would be overthrown, perhaps by United Nations Action. The Pope bided his time. By 1951 the climate was changing. The Cold War became more and more frigid, and the Pope's life-long anti-communism, which had led him into thorny paths regarding his relationship with the Axis, now seemed justified.[35]

In 1952 the 35th World Eucharistic Congress was celebrated in Barcelona, in spite of French protests, attributed by *Ya* to the 'international masonic conspiracy'. Mgr. Angel Herrera celebrated a special Mass for the Spanish militants of Catholic Action. Franco addressed the Congress and 'consecrated Spain to the Holy Sacrament'.[36]

It was the United States who finally clinched the issue by their friendly approaches to Franco. When the Concordat was signed it seemed appropriate that the Spanish representative at the Holy See was no longer Ruiz Giménez but Castiella, who had sworn allegiance to the person of Adolf Hitler in 1941.[37] Ruiz Giménez had worked ceaselessly for the Concordat, and was rewarded by a cabinet place in 1951 – the Ministry of Education. Negotiations had not always been easy. The Pope had to keep a careful eye on opinion elsewhere. In 1950 he had criticized press censorship, but the Francoists sighed with relief when it was made clear that His Holiness predictably was not referring to Spain but to the Communist world.[38] Freedom of the press meant of course freedom of the Catholic press. This was the era of Arias Salgado, and his rigid press censorship in Spain.

While Ruiz Giménez was engaged in diplomacy, Angel Herrera was staging a spectacular comeback in his new guise as Bishop of Málaga. He eulogised Franco over Radio Vatican in June 1950.[39] Spain had rejected the false principles of the French revolution he said – he was probably not conversant with the text of Franco's first pronunciamiento in July 1936 which had invoked 'la trilogía fraternidad, libertad e igualdad'.[40] Martín Artajo was also very vocal. He stated in *Ya* in June 1951[41] that Spain had more essential liberties than any other country, home, work, education and freedom of movement(sic). The 'secondary' freedoms of speech, press, party were unsuited to Spaniards, who were given to 'libertinaje'.

The 'Catholic Action Concordat' became a reality on 27 August 1953, and the special role of Catholic Action was rewarded by Clause 34 – ensuring its complete freedom to carry out its apostolate without hindrance from the State.

THE CONCORDAT

THE IMPORTANCE OF THE CONCORDAT

The 1953 Concordat replaced that of 1851, and was in many ways more satisfactory both for Church and regime. It largely ratified the post-civil war status quo which had been established by the *convenio* of 1941, granting the Church control of education and exclusive right to proselytise as the sole State religion. Freedom of worship existed in theory[42] but it was confined to private observances and all non-Catholic 'cults' (only the Roman denomination was deemed 'religion') were forbidden to advertise services or display crosses etc. outside their churches. Obligatory Catholic instruction at all schools was re-affirmed, as was the Church's power in the fields of all education and censorship. Divorce was still illegal, and although non-Catholics could obtain civil marriage it was extremely difficult to achieve. The Church enjoyed large fiscal benefits, and the State would pay tax-free clerical stipends, and continue to subsidize the reconstruction of Church property destroyed during the Civil War. An elaborate scheme for this purpose had been in existence under Mariano Puigdollers of the ACNP.[43] Clergy were to be exempt from military service and if charged with any offence would be tried in special courts. This was one of the clauses which at the time perhaps would appear of lesser importance but later assumed great significance. Another concerned Franco's *patronato* with regard to the appointment of bishops. It was of course confirmed, and Franco was given the final say in who was appointed and where he should have his diocese — this last of particular significance in Cataluña and the Basque country. However, this right was confined to residential bishops and archbishops, and was not applicable to: (1) titular bishops appointed as auxiliaries; and (2) apostolic administrators appointed to cover dioceses temporarily. These appointments, being of lesser importance, were made directly by the Vatican, thus avoiding the often lengthy procedure necessary when a permanent bishop was appointed. This apparently small point was another which was to assume immense political significance fifteen years later. The final sanctification of the crusade of Franco was the prayer for *Ducem nostrum Franciscum* to be said at Mass.

The Spanish hierarchy greeted the Concordat with great satisfaction. The Church had virtually equal status with the secular power, an unprecedented state of affairs in the modern world. However, there was some cause for disquiet among a minority within the Church. The economic link with the regime was so tight that the Church would find it extremely difficult to speak with an independent voice. Some clerics thought this would make their pastoral mission difficult. They wished to 'rechristianize' the defeated working class, but the Concordat merely emphasized yet again that the Church had thrown in its lot completely with the victorious ruling oligarchy. It would be very difficult for the Church not to be tied down by its link with Franco, but the converse was surely untrue. Franco was unlikely to be affected by Church opinion. He would pursue whatever course he thought fit.

THE CATHOLIC WORKERS' MOVEMENT

Article 34 of the Concordat protected Catholic Action and allowed it freedom to conduct its activities without the tight police scrutiny to which other organizations were subject. This was again on the surface perfectly acceptable to Franco. After all, the Catholic Action movement had been a prop for the regime during and after the Civil War,[44] and its ACNP leadership had to a large extent been responsible for the Concordat. Catholic Action was nominally under the control of the pro-Franco hierarchy, and its periodicals *Ecclesia, Signo*, etc. were not likely to come out with criticism of the regime. However, this happy state of affairs was not to last.

In 1947 Cardinal Plá had formed a group within Catholic Action whose function it was to spread Christian ideals in the sphere of labour. The organization was called *Hermandades Obreras de Acción Católica.* It was not a success at first. The working class, already repressed by the vertical sindicatos run by the Falange were unlikely to respond favourably to advances from the clerical quarter either. But Catholic Action had always been 'social' in outlook, even in the days of Acción Popular when the social function of Catholicism was interpreted as a paternalistic corporativism designed to counter socialism. Since then, fascism had been defeated in Europe, and the authoritarianism advocated in the thirties had been diluted into 'Christian Democracy'. Ex-fascist Italy, Germany and Vichy France now had flourishing Christian Democrat parties, and Catholic trade unions were growing up, co-existing with the socialist-orientated unions. This was bound to affect Spain in the fifties, when the economic *apertura* was already discernible. In 1954 Catholic Action issued a statement condemning the low wages suffered by the majority of workers and demanding an increase in the minimum wage. The HOAC began to increase its support under leaders like Robirosa, Malagón and Cardijn. A powerful youth branch was set up by Cardijn the *Juventud Obrera Católica.* The significance of these organizations was that they were the only legal workers' groups outside the Sindicatos and the government was reluctant to move against them for fear of the bad propaganda effect of breaking the Concordat.

The Falange was now becoming aware of the threat that the HOAC and JOC might present to their syndical monopoly. They began to make disgruntled noises. Cardinal Plá himself became disturbed by the vision of what HOAC may lead to. In 1957 he tightened up clerical discipline, giving bishops more power of surveillance over rebellious young clergy.[45]

HOAC progress was slow, and 1955 saw the emergence of a more militant Catholic movement, the *Frente de Liberación Popular* founded by Julio Cerón Ayuso. Its manifesto demanded violent seizure of power by the working class, suppression of private ownership of industry, replacement of the army by people's militias, nationalization of banks and the foundation of a 'classless society'.[46] The Church hierarchy were horrified that such an organization should be — at least nominally — Catholic in inspiration. The 'Felipes' found a brilliant propagandist in Ignacio Fernández de Castro, who can be compared with many modern Catholics especially in Latin America, who interpret the gospel as advocating a revolutionary movement to emancipate the poor. He has stated that the inspiration of these militants is broadly Christian rather than Catholic, and states that many workers in the HOAC, JOC, FLP, etc., are former anarchists converted in prison ostensibly to Catholicism but really to militant revolutionary Christianity — an ironic example of a 'counterproductive' activity on the part of the regime-backed Church.[47] In 1959 Cerón Ayuso was brought to trial and given eight years for military rebellion. He was defended by Gil Robles, who had returned to Spain and begun a new career as defence lawyer for anti-Franco militants.[48]

The Falange were now seriously worried. The HOAC openly contested the 1960 elections for the sindicatos, and Cardinal Plá objected that the harassment of HOAC members was against Article 34 of the Concordat. He had clearly decided that he had to support the Catholic workers' movement if the working class were to be prevented from returning to anticlerical 'marxism'. Franco, however, also saw a danger of 'liberalism' in the HOAC and backed the repressive measures taken by the sindicato boss Solís Ruíz. But the struggle went on. The HOAC, JOC and FLP were prominent in the organization of the massive strikes of 1962, working together with marxist workmates in the emerging *Comisiones Obreras.* In May 1962 the president of HOAC Teofilo Pérez Rey was fined 50,000 pesetas for illegal propaganda in support of the Asturian miners' strike.[49] Even *Ecclesia*, organ of the hierarchy-dominated upper echelons of Catholic Action, defended the legality of HOAC against attacks by Emilio Romero in the Falangist '*Pueblo*'. In twenty years the role of Catholic Action had been transformed. To be a Catholic militant no longer meant to be a Francoist.

Catholic Action had moved left not only in the work sphere but also in the field of journalism. Joaquin Ruíz Giménez was removed as Minister of Education following the 1950 Úniversity disturbances, and since then has become the spokesman for an outward-looking, more liberal, even democratic form of Catholic political commitment, later founding a progressive review *Cuadernos para el Diálogo*. One of the reasons for this liberalization of Catholic Action must be found in the rise to power of a tougher, less amorphous and economically more powerful pressure group – Opus Dei.

OPUS DEI

ORIGINS OF OPUS DEI

Father Ángel Ayala, S. J., founded the ACNP in 1909 in reaction against Canalejas. The Sociedad Sacerdotal de la Santa Cruz y del Opus Dei was founded in October 1928 under the dictatorship of Primo de Rivera. It can therefore hardly be said to have been a reaction against the policies of a government. On the contrary, the Opus was not inspired by opposition to authority, but by support for Primo's administration. The founder of Opus, Fr. Jose María Escrivá de Balaguer, supported the concessions made by Primo to clericalism, and was appalled at the hostility the regime brought about in intellectual circles.

Escrivá was born in a pueblo (Barbastro) in a backward province (Huesca) and clearly was disturbed when he reached the úniversity in Zaragoza to discover that perhaps Spain was not quite the Catholic country he thought it to be. University life seemed dominated by 'foreign' liberalism and republicanism and the integrist-minded young priest (he was ordained in 1925) pondered upon the problem of how to reconquer Spain for the traditional Church. He was undoubtedly influenced by the elitism of ACNP, ironically, since this organization was Jesuit-based, and the Opus and the Society were later to become bitter opponents. Escrivá did in fact teach in the Jesuit school of journalism associated with Angel Herrera's *El Debate*.[50] He noted that the liberal intellectual leadership was dominated by the ideals of the *Institución Libre de Enseñanza* and its associated organizations, such as the *Junta para la Ampliación de Estudios*, the 'Resi' (*Residencia de Estudiantes*), founded by Giner de los Ríos, and the Madrid *Instituto-Escuela*. As a good follower of Piux X, he detected the influence of Freemasonry behind this efficient network of liberal institutions, with their strong influence on the education of youth, which Escrivá wished to restore to the Church. Clearly, the amorphous Catholic Action, with

20

its 'social' ideas was not the answer — better to create an anti-masonry which would infiltrate education and counter the subversive heresies of liberalism. Escrivá was not the first to think of this means of doing battle with the enemies of the Church. Pope Pius X, with Cardinals Benigni and Merry del Val, had already set up in 1909 an organization known as *Sodalitium Pianum*, a secret 'police' which would root out from the Church any heresies and modernist doctrines, condemned by the encyclical *Pascendi Gregis* of 1907.[51] The 'S.P.' was particularly active in France, where it was known as *La Sapinière*, and became the scourge of the French modernist disciples of Alfred Loisy who attempted to reinterpret Catholicism in terms of the modern world of science.

The coming of the Republic saw the birth of *Acción Española* — rabidly monarchist and antidemocratic — a further source of inspiration for the thoughtful Escrivá. The Opus itself was still a small group of university men of like mind, and during the Republic it expanded little. Its first residence opened in 1934 in Madrid, and a feminine branch had been founded, but it was the Civil War which gave the Opus its great opportunity.[52]

'CAMINO'

The Francoist year of victory also saw the publication of *Camino*, the handbook consisting of 999 maxims which has become the breviary of the Opus faithful. The theological content of the maxims is superficial, indeed banal, and the real significance of the book lies in its general ethos. It contains the usual clichés regarding the necessity for faith, prayer, sanctity, charity, etc., but far more significantly, it is a call for leadership, indeed it uses the Spanish jargon of the day in its insistence on *caudillaje*. For example, Maxims 16 and 24 use this term, urging members to become leaders and to rise above the common herd. It seeks to create an elite, to transform Spain 'de arriba-abajo'. In this it echoes the elitism of Maura, Maeztú and the ACNP, and introduces an element akin to the Nietzschean concept of the 'superman' fashionable in the fascism of the day. The originality of *Camino* is that it combines the most intransigent integrism with an espousal of material progress more typical of northern protestant Europe — Weber's 'industrial ethic' in fact. The previous integrist movements within the Church had condemned capitalism and preached a return to a mediaeval feudalism uncorrupted by the false ideas of the Enlightenment. Escrivá combines the clerical authoritarianism of Pius IX, with the profit motive of Henry Ford. It is a strange combination, but it was to prove an unbeatable one in the Spanish context.

The Opus could only germinate in the context of the victory of 'fascism' but the decline of the Falange lead to an ideological gap which Catholic Action was not strong enough to fill in the long term. Francoism needed the Opus Dei, but the time was not yet ripe for the ideological take-over.

THE OPUS, THE UNIVERSITY AND CSIC

Franco's first Minister of Education was Pedro Sáinz Rodríguez, formerly a leading member of Calvo Sotelo's *Renovación Española* and one of the *Acción Española* group of monarchists. The Church had got on well with the Minister, and were well set on their recapture of control over education. However, Sáinz Rodríguez quarrelled bitterly with the Falange over clerical education and was forced to resign.[58] The Church passed some anxious moments lest a militant falangist be appointed. They need not have worried. The new minister was a compromise candidate, José Ibáñez Martín, a typical 'new shirt', and an ex-member of CEDA and an ACNP militant. His appointment was a stroke of luck for Opus Dei, for he was a close friend of José María Albareda Herrera, one of the original members of Opus. On 24 November 1939 they collaborated in the creation of the *Consejo Superior de Investigaciones Científicas* (CSIC).

The CSIC replaced the *Junta para Ampliación de Estudios* and the Republican *Fundación Nacional de Investigaciones Científicas* and became a sort of parody of these institutions. The purpose of CSIC was, first, to undo the work achieved by these earlier organizations and, second, to substitute the new victorious ideology of the 'Cruzada'. It chose as its emblem the 'Tree of Knowledge' (*El Árbol de la Ciencia*) of Ramón Lull, and, like that mediaeval educationist, the CSIC personally regarded themselves as missionaries whose task it was to propagate the true doctrines of authoritarian Christianity but with emphasis placed upon learning and science. The CSIC was a State organization and therefore presented the Opus Dei with its great opportunity to infiltrate the machinery of the regime itself. Albareda was Secretary General of CSIC from 1939 until his death in 1966. During that time an enormous number of Opus members and sympathisers passed through its tutelage. Like its predecessor, the *Junta para Ampliación*, the CSIC were responsible for the allocation of grants for higher education. The Opus Dei were, therefore, able to use this means to select people favourable to their ideology and thereby further their aim of building up an elite leadership in Francoist Spain.

While the Catholic Action group were engaged in political activity, the Opus were at this early stage involved, above all, in the educational field. The CSIC became the 'springboard' from which the Opus could attempt the conquest of university chairs. Here they came up against two main groups of rivals: Catholic Action itself in the form of the Jesuit-based ACNP, and, of course, the Falange. The system of obtaining chairs was that of the *Oposiciones.* In 1943 the *Ley de Ordenación Universitaria* gave the Minister of Education the power to nominate three of the five members of the Tribunal which would super-vise the tests required for selection for a university chair. The presence in the Ministry of Ibáñez Martín meant that the Opus Dei were able to obtain a large number of university chairs. Among those successful in obtaining important chairs during the forties were Calvo Serer, Pérez Embid, Antonio Fontán, Alvaro d'Ors, Alberto Ullastres and López Rodó. The period of Opus ascendancy in the university world was to end when Ibáñez Martín was replaced as Minister of Education in 1951 by Ruíz Giménez. By that time, however, the Opus strength was such that the tactic was changed, and it became clear to the Opus that their future in the university lay not only within the State system, but also in founding a separate university of their own.

ORGANIZATION OF OPUS DEI

The first offical recognition granted to the movement was in 1941 when they were recognized by the Bishop of Madrid-Alcalá, the extremist Eijó y Garay, as a 'Pía Unión'. However, Escrivá aspired much higher. In 1946 he moved to Rome accompanied by Alvaro del Portillo who was to play a crucial role in the future of Opus Dei. In Rome Escrivá and Portillo made many friends including important members of the Curia such as Mgr. Tardini and the then Mgr. Montini (later Pope Paul VI). It was the aim of Escrivá that the Opus should transcend the status of a mere association of the Catholic Action type, without becoming a religious order since this would inhibit its activities in the world. Some new form of organization was obviously needed to fit the precise requirements. The answer came in February 1947 when Pope Pius XII issued the Bull *Provida Mater Ecclesia* which created a new form of religious organization, the secular institute. These were to be half-way between religious orders and Catholic 'field' organizations. Members of secular institutes could be either priests or laity. The priest members took the normal vows of regular clergy whereas lay members also took vows thereby distinguishing themselves from members of Catholic Action or pious unions. However, the nature of the vows taken by lay members has led to some ambiguity in interpretation. These are regarded as 'private' rather than 'public'. This distinction is most important in the sense that the vows are therefore not permanent and can be renounced. It must be stressed, however, that even lay members of Opus take the vow of celibacy, if they come into the category of numerarii.

Something must be said about what actually constitutes membership of Opus Dei. As befits an elitist organization, there are various categories: celibate members, clerical or lay,[54] are divided into numerarii and oblati. Numerarii possess a university degree, often live in community, but wear no distinctive clothing. An interesting requirement demanded of these high-ranking members of the association is that they must be fit and possess no physical deformity. The lower category are those who do not fulfil the requirements to become numerarii. They are celibate but do not live in community. Strict distinction is maintained between the two groups and promotion is very rare. *Caudillos* demanded by Escrivá in *Camino* are found not only among the numerarii but among the supernumerarii. These also must posess university degrees but are allowed to marry. Perhaps the most important category of all is that of the Cooperatores. These make no vows but are merely loosely attached to the Opus and participate in activities such as retreats, etc., and have Opus priests as Confessors. It is perhaps to these sympathisers that the Opus owes most. The Opus has been called a sort of 'secret society' – although 'discretion' is the term used in *Camino* – and this aspect is especially important with regard to these sympathisers. It is virtually impossible to find out precisely who is or who is not a sympathiser of Opus Dei.[55] The rise of the Opus in the fifties and sixties owed much to the help of these Cooperatores or 'fellow travellers'.

THE OPUS BREAK-THROUGH

The arrival of Ruíz Giménez in 1951 brought to an end the period of Opus ascendancy in the State Universities, and the following year the Opus set up the Estudio General de Navarra. This was a university-type institution but for the moment could not aspire to recognition as a university, since the 1943 Law reaffirmed the State monopoly of university education. Jesuits had experienced similar difficulty with their university at Deusto and in 1928 Escrivá was witness to the massive campaign organized by the then liberal universities against the proposed recognition of Deusto by the Primo de Rivera government. The 1953 Concordat allowed the Church to form educational establishmenta at any level, but the Opus group were prepared to bide their time before achieving recognition for the Estudio General. In the meantime, the Navarra institution was closely linked to Escrivá's own *alma mater*, the university of Zaragoza where the Opus held many chairs.

The attention of the Opus was now directed more broadly at the world of journalism, business, banking and, ultimately, government. In 1951 Admiral Luis Carrero Blanco, according to some a Cooperator of the Opus, but according to Ynfante a full supernumerarius, was appointed sub-secretary of the Presidencia del Gobierno. This appointment marks the beginning of Opus involvement in government and also the close link it was to strengthen with the person of Franco himself since Carrero Blanco was an old comrade-in-arms of the General. At about this time members of the Opus also achieved firm control of the Banco Popular Español, thanks largely to a syndicate of shareholders which included the Valls Taberner family. The Banco Popular Español was to fulfil the function in the economic field which the CSIC had done in the academic. It was the main 'spring-board' for Opus capitalistic expansionism. The Banco Popular created Esfina (*Sociedad Española de Estudios Financieros*) to search out likely sources of profitable investment. One of its most significant acquisitions was the Credit Andorra through which lucrative trade in foreign exchange could be carried out. The world of publishing also became a target. In 1948 the publishing house Rialp was founded by Calvo Serer and Pérez Embid, and in 1951 SARPE (*Sociedad Anónima de Revistas Publicaciones y Edicionas*) was founded to acquire periodicals, the first significant one being the weekly *Actualidad Española*.

1953 saw the birth of a new 'catch phrase', 'tercera fuerza', the invention of Rafael Calvo Serer, the leading Opus ideologue. It was used in an article in the Rightist *Les Ecrits de Paris* and led to his dismissal from his post in the CSIC and from the editorship of the CSIC journal *Arbor*. However, he was allowed to retain his chair at the university of Madrid because clearly the regime secretly welcomed this new political element. Escrivá and the Opus Dei have always denied that they have any political ideology. They insist that their members are of many political persuasions. In practice, this has not been the case, at least until very recently. Opus political ideology has consistently been largely that outlined by Calvo Serer in this article. 1953 was, of course, a year of triumph for Catholic Action. Also, the Falangists, 150,000 of whom acclaimed Franco in the Real Madrid football stadium in October 1953, were still a powerful political force and dominated the bureaucracy of the regime. In order to achieve hegemony Opus had to attack the other two principal pressure groups within Francoism. It must be said that the third force advocated by Calvo Serer was ideologically on the extreme right. Both the Falange and the so-called 'Christian Democrats' of Catholic Action and ACNP, were attacked. The Falange were labelled 'radical and republican'; *Pueblo* and *Arriba* were especially mentioned as sowing the seeds of 'leftism' and Falangists referred to as 'opportunistic revolutionaries'. The Catholic Action group were villified for their toleration of the anti-Christian ideology defeated in 1939. The clerical newspaper *Ya* was considered the organ of this attitude, and Martín Artajo and, naturally, Ruíz Giménez singled out for criticism. A third force was required based upon Catholicism, monarchy and other traditional Spanish values. In short, Calvo Serer is preaching a new integrism. However, it is, of course, integrism Opus style, i.e. still violently opposed to democracy combined with 'laissez-faire' economics and the ideology of 'desarrollo'. Calvo Serer had previously written in 1949 a book entitled *España Sin Problema* in which he advocated a return to the values of the Crusade which he considered had been abandoned by certain Falangist intellectuals, like Antonio Tovar and Pedro Laín Entralgo. Calvo Serer's book was, in fact, a reply to Laín's *España Como Problema*. In 1954 appeared Calvo's *España después de los Tratados*, a pamphlet restating this new aggressive Opus standpoint. Calvo Serer was, therefore, responsible more than anyone else for the setting out of a corpus of political doctrine which was soon to be put into practice. The debate concerning the 'tercera fuerza' took place at the time of the new relationship which was developing between Spain and the USA. Calvo Serer advocated the integration of Spain into the Western capitalist world. Therefore, although an enemy of *political* liberalism, he advocated an extreme form of *economic* liberalism and it is here that we see the paradox of the so-called 'liberalization' of Francoism. Calvo Serer criticized the 'totalitarianism' of the Falange as inimical to the prosperity of Spain, whilst at the same time he utterly opposed any form of relaxation of the authoritarian nature of Franco Spain. It is a common fallacy to state that the Opus ascendancy and decline of the Falange represent liberalization in the political sense. The Opus were merely anxious that the Spanish ruling class should benefit from the development of foreign trade and a market economy and wanted to end the period of isolation.

In 1956 Spain was torn by crises. There was a wave of strikes and the universities were the scene of violent clashes between Falangists and their opponents. The final attempt of the Falange to gain permanent control over the regime failed with the rejection by Franco of Arrese's Leyes Fundamentales. The first force, the Falange, was losing ground, the second force, the 'Christian Democrats', of Catholic Action, were slowly moving away from the regime, the third force, the Opus Dei, now had their opportunity to establish themselves. The government of February 1957 contained eight Ministers who were either members or sympathisers of Opus Dei including two celibate numerarii, Alberto Ullastres and Laureano López Rodó, although, strictly speaking, the latter was not really a Minister but Technical Secretary to Carrero Blanco at the Presidencia del Gobierno. The results of Opus intervention in government are well-known — the Stabilization Plan, the Collective Bargaining Law, etc. That economic liberalization certainly did not mean political relaxation can be seen from the appointment of General Alonso Vega as Minister of the Interior. Carrero Blanco and Alonso Vega provided the hard line repression under which the younger Opus group led by Ullastres and López Rodó could develop their economic policies. In 1962 and 1965 Opus representation in the government was further expanded and it was now apparent to all Spaniards that the denials made by members of the society regarding their lack of political ambition were not to be taken seriously. The two López's became household names. They were an interesting contrast. López Rodó, a celibate numerarius and Gregorio López Bravo, a married supernumerarius and father of a large family. The inauguration of the first Plan de Desarrollo in 1964 was the complete victory of Opus economic policies.

In 1962 the Opus finally achieved their own university when the degrees granted by the Estudio General de Navarra were recognized by the State, though the institution had been recognized as a Universidad de la Iglesia in 1960. Prominent in its curriculum were journalism and business studies. The latter was especially important and the IESE (*Instituto de Estudios Superiores de la Empresa*) which had established a link with the Harvard Business School, became a breeding ground for the new elite of Spanish neo-capitalism.

When one looks at the spectacular advance of Opus Dei from 1939 to 1964 one is once again struck by the way in which it took the organizations left behind by its defeated enemies in 1939, and distorted and inverted them. The organization of the Opus Dei itself with its secrecy and hierarchy reflects Freemasonry. Its integrist elitism reflects the liberal elitism of the *Institucion Libre de Enseñanza*. The CSIC

27

reflects the *Junta para Ampliacion*; the *Colegios Mayores* reflect Giner's *Residencia de Estudiantes* and the *Instituto Ramiro Maeztú* reflects the *Instituto-Escuela*. Opus Dei appears a mirror parody of the progressive intelligentsia defeated in the Civil War.

SPAIN AND VATICAN II

THE JOHANNINE ENCYCLICALS

On 9 October 1958 Franco Spain lost one of its closest allies with the death of Pope Pius XII. He was expected to be succeeded by Cardinal Montini, a friend of Opus Dei who might have been expected to continue the friendly attitude of the Vatican towards the Spanish regime, although in 1962 the Cardinal, then Archbishop of Milan, was to clash publicly with Franco.[56] As it turned out, Montini had to wait five years before ascending the throne of St. Peter, for the unexpected happened and Cardinal Angelo Giuseppe Roncalli was elected Pope John XXIII. At first Catholic traditionalists were not worried. Although personally very different from his predecessor, the new Pope was regarded as a conservative. His first speech contained the statement that salvation is possible only through the Roman Church. He exalted the contemplative life and condemned the 'heresy of action'. However, when his first Encyclical was issued many elements in the Catholic world were astonished. It appeared in May 1961 and was called *Mater et Magistra* and was basically an historical survey of Catholic teaching in social matters from Leo XIII and *Rerum Novarum* down to current issues. It spoke of poverty and social discontent but unlike virtually every previous Encyclical on social matters it omitted the customary tirade against atheistic Communism. It was greeted with concern by Catholic conservatives throughout the world. William F. Buckley in the US described it as trivial[57] but it was ambiguous enough to be greeted with approval by Opus Dei. Ullastres in his famous speech of 1 June in Barcelona after a diatribe against 'progresismo' stated that *Mater et Magistra* reaffirmed traditional Catholic teaching against liberalism – in the socio-political sense, of course. *Mater et Magistra* seemed to provide something for everyone. As far as Spain was concerned, an ominous note was struck in the message sent by His Holiness in September 1961 to the Bishop of Barcelona Modrego Casaus. In it the Pope lamented the deplorable and cruel Civil War; the term 'Crusade' was not used.

The real bombshell was the publication in April 1963 of the Encyclical *Pacem in Terris*. This document gave less scope for mixed interpretation. It advocated peaceful co-existence, freedom of speech, freedom of communication, freedom of association and basic civil rights including the right for a people to choose those who govern them in the temporal sphere. It condemned societies which repress these freedoms and also those who suppress freedoms of language, culture, etc., of minorities. Many liberal Catholics, who now formed part of the opposition in Spain, seriously considered that the Encyclical was referring specifically to Spain. As for the hierarchy, they greeted its publication with stunned silence. Pope John died two months after its publication and in his End of Year message Franco spoke the customary words of sorrow but did not mention the Encyclical and much of his speech indeed contradicted it.[58] Of even greater significance than the Encyclical was the opening of the first session of the Second Vatican Council in October 1962.

THE SPANISH BISHOPS AND VATICAN II

Many Spanish bishops attended the deliberations at Rome. Their performance can hardly be said to have been particularly auspicious. Inevitably, they found themselves lining up with the reactionary element. A typical speech was that of the Archbishop of Santiago de Compostela, Cardinal Quiroga y Palacios. He had been brought up on the traditional integrist teaching regarding the evils of liberalism. He asked the Council why these doctrines should now be revised. He saw no reason for this. This intransigent attitude was echoed by the Archbishop of Burgos, the Bishop of Siguenza, Mgr. Castaín, and others. The Spanish hierarchy were particularly vocal in their condemnation of freedom of worship during the Council debate on that subject. One of the most prestigious of Spanish church leaders, Cardinal Benjamín de Arriba y Castro made the point that freedom of worship must be suppressed in those countries like Spain where Catholicism is the leading religion.[59] Only the Catholic Church has the right to preach the Gospel, he said, though clearly the Spanish Bishops favoured freedom of religion in non-Catholic countries. One of the least dignified episodes in the entire proceedings was the speech by the aged Bishop of Lérida, Mgr. Aurelio Pino Gómez who fulminated against socialism stating that private property is a way of honouring God, and that there could never be any redemption for non-believers (i.e. non-Catholics) who could look forward only to hell fire. The assembled Council greeted the speech with laughter and the microphone had to be taken away from the old cleric.[60] It must be remembered that of the

Spanish Bishops a large proportion were over 75 years old and over 90% had been ordained before the Civil War. However, the unedifying Spanish interventions on the floor of the Council Chamber do not represent the whole story. The Pontificate of John XXIII and Vatican II had a profound effect in Spain and indeed began a rift in the clergy which was to assume definitive importance. The aged Bishops were counterbalanced by a young clergy who had no personal memories of the Civil War. Many of these young priests were inspired by the spirit of Vatican II, and they often found themselves at odds with their spiritual superiors. Already in 1960 339 Basque priests had spoken out for more freedom and many of the younger clergy often involved in HOAC and JOC were to be found positively supporting strikes in 1962. For the moment the division was largely between a leftward moving clergy and an entrenched reactionary Episcopate. However, even some bishops were caught up by the spirit of the Council and even Cardinal Plá supported Pope John's advocacy of the right to strike.[61] During the 1962 strikes Bishop Gúrpide Beope of Bilbao, normally a typical member of the conservative faction, stated that one of the causes for the industrial unrest was low pay, rather than the oft-quoted 'international Communist agitators'. He was supported by the Archbishop of Seville, Cardinal Bueno y Monreal, thought by many to be Cardinal Plá's likely successor as Primate.

The most famous voice among senior Spanish progressive Churchmen was that of Dom Aureli Escarré, Benedictine Abbot of Montserrat, who did much to end the ban on the Catalan language through his monthly review *Serra d'Or*. In November 1963 the Abbot gave an interview to *Le Monde* regarding the forthcoming celebrations for '25 years of peace'. Invoking the spirit of *Pacem in Terris*, he stated that Francoism was really celebrating 25 years of victory, adding that a people has the right to choose its rulers and that Press freedom was necessary. He spoke of the need for democracy and liberty and ended with the amazing statement 'Colectivamente nuestros hombres políticos no son cristianos'. This was probably the most unequivocal attack on the Franco regime yet delivered by a senior Spanish cleric.[62] It brought a heated reply from one of Franco's closest supporters Dom Escarré's fellow Benedictine Fray Pérez de Urbel, Abbot of the Valle de los Caídos. Another old friend of Franco, Cardinal Antonutti, former Nuncio in Madrid, attempted to obtain the dissolution of the Montserrat monastery and its absorption by that of the Valley of the Fallen. The new Pope, Paul VI, refused, but Dom Escarré who had been removed for 'health reasons' following his attack on Franco, was forced to retire. Unfortunately, for the regime, his successor Dom Just Cassiá stated his intention to continue the line of his predecessor which he proceeded to do. The Bishops themselves, however, remained solidly behind the regime and it was left for the moment to the lower clergy to put into practise the spirit of the Council.

THE POSTCONCILIAR SITUATION

The effect of Vatican II in Spain was traumatic. The Council was seen to represent a new spirit in the Church and the events that followed it seemed to indicate to many Catholics that the modernist/integrist controversy dating back over 100 years had finally been settled in favour of modernism. To a non-Catholic this seems strange, especially in view of the publicity given to the Encyclical *Humanae Vitae* (1968) which seemed a reactionary statement. However, within the Church the more liberal attitude was on the advance, and Vatican II was profoundly significant, more for what it seemed to epitomise than for its practical results.[63]

The Spanish bishops could hardly attack the Council openly or the new Pope, Cardinal Montini, in spite of his clash with Franco in 1962.[64] Montini who had become Pope Paul VI in 1963 had presided over all but the first session of the Council. His policy statement on social issues came with the Encyclical *Populorum Progressio* (1967). It was largely devoted to the 'third world', spoke in favour of independence for colonial countries and denounced imperialism. It called on Catholics to fulfil their role in the attack on poverty. Franco stated in his End-of-Year message in 1967 that *Populorum Progressio* 'ha venido a sostener con su doctrina las soluciones que en España están en vigor desde hace treinta años'.[65] The words had a hollow ring. The Vatican was about to abandon the Franco regime.

The split within Spanish Catholicism had widened significantly in 1966. One of the most important examples can be seen in the crisis within Catholic Action. The movement was now rent between the progressive laity and the conservative bishops. Titular head of the movement, the Cardinal Primate Plá y Deniel was dying and leadership was *de facto* in the hands of the Archbishop of Madrid, who was president of the CEAS (Comisión Episcopal de Apostolado Seglar) which co-ordinated all branches of the lay movement — Catholic Action, the Jesuit-led Congregaciones Marianas, the Pías Uniones, etc. On the death of the fanatical Mgr. Eijó y Garay in 1963, the see of Madrid was raised to an Archbishopric and the Archbishop of Zaragoza, Mgr. Casimiro Morcillo González moved to the capital. He was described at the time by some as a liberal[66] but his actions were to belie this. He became one of the leaders of the struggle of the reactionary Bishops to maintain strong ties with Francoism. His role in the Catholic Action crisis began when the lay element demanded that the spirit of Vatican II be followed criticizing the attitude of the hierarchy and advocating more control by the laity. The annual Congress, the 'Jornadas Nacionales de Acción Católica', was suspended and many liberal delegates, among them representatives of HOAC and JOC were sanctioned. The only compromise offered by Archbishop Morcillo was that the lay president of ACE should be elected rather than appointed.

1967 saw the referendum regarding the Organic Law. The bishops urged support for Franco. The laity and younger priests protested. Bishop Gúrpide Beope of Bilbao suspended all HOAC and JOC members in his diocese who had signed a manifesto urging a 'No' vote. Many Catholic Action publications were seized under the new 'liberal' press law. *Signo* and *Juventud Obrera* were frequently sequestrated and *Aún*, edited by young Jesuits, was wound up definitively on the advice of Morcillo following an article *En busca de una Iglesia conciliar*.

The clash came to a head in June 1967 when the Jornadas Nacionales had to select delegates for the World Catholic Action Congress (World Council of Secular Apostolate) in Rome. An extraordinary situation emerged. The official delegation selected by the hierarchy completely excluded all delegates from the HOAC, JOC and Vanguardias Obreras. One of its prominent members, however, was a Madrid lawyer, Blas Piñar, who was embarking upon a career as a leader of rightist extremism, founding the journal *Fuerza Nueva* on 14 January 1967. The official delegation was rejected by the rank and file who sent a second delegation under Joaquin Ruíz Giménez.

Further controversy surrounded the favourable response in *Signo* to an invitation to dialogue from Santiago Carrillo, leader of the Communist Party. The entire editorial staff were dismissed.

The demands for more power for the laity were largely rejected, when a new constitution for ACE was approved, by the VI Episcopal Conference. However, 25% of the Bishops voted against, in support of the laity, much to the consternation of Cardinal Quiroga, President of the Conference in the absence of the aged Primate Plá. The end result was that the attempt by the liberal element to take over organization of Catholic Action had failed. Wholesale resignations followed. Membership stood at one million in 1966, but dropped astonishingly by 1972 to a mere 100,000 (Survey by Bishop Dorado Soto of Guadix-Baza).[67]

Vatican II had seen the rift between the reactionary hierarchy and the younger priests widen. Sanctions against priests became commonplace, and all over Spain many of the clergy now identified themselves with the workers' cause. A special prison was opened for priests at Zamora, since the Concordat stipulated priests should be treated separately. Many events took place that achieved great symbolic importance Among these was the sit-in at the Capuchin convent at Sarriá and the similar action at Bilbao, where the episcopal offices were taken over by 40 priests on 18 August 1968 – the culmination of a long struggle between left-wing Basque clergy and the reactionary bishop Pablo Gúrpide in which the bishop had consistently castigated priests who supported strikes. Various episodes took place in which priests refused to say Mass unless the red-and-yellow national flag was removed. Space precludes mention of more than one or two such examples of clashes between clergy and authorities. The funeral of Ex-Bishop Mateo Múgica was turned into an anti-Franco demonstration, imprisoned priests went on hunger-strike as a protest against police brutality in Bilbao, etc.

Especially significant is the fact that a split in the monolithic wall of the pro-Franco Bishops was now appearing. Whereas previously the activities against the regime were largely confined to younger priests, liberal voices now began to be heard among the Bishops themselves. The 20 votes against the new Catholic Action constitution, which failed to modernise the structure, came from a new emergent group of liberal Bishops. Fr. Joaquín Gomis in *Episcopado y clero en la crisis posconciliar*, an article which appeared in *El Ciervo* in October 1966,[68] traces the history of three groups among the episcopate: (1) the 20 or so liberals, who became bishops during the time of Nuncio Mgr. Riberi; (2) a middle group of neo-conservatives elevated during the time of Nuncio Mgr. Antonutti; (3) the majority of reactionary old-timers, ordained before the Civil War, whose numbers were gradually becoming depleted by death. 62 bishops had been ordained before 1936 according to '*Vida Nueva*' in 1967, and the average age of the hierarchy (66) was far above the world and European average.

Liberal statements from the Spanish Bishops had previously been few and far between, and when they did occur they were extremely muted. The late sixties saw a change. The voice of episcopal protest against the repressive regime came geographically speaking from an unexpected quarter – not from the Basque provinces nor from Cataluña but from Spain's 'deep south' – the 'latifundio' areas of Andalucía.

Mgr. José María Cirarda Lachiando was auxiliary Bishop of Seville and Mgr. Antonio Añoveros Ataún Bishop of Cádiz-Ceuta. They spoke out against the low wages of agricultural labourers. Bishop Añoveros pointed out that the day of the 'bracero' was far from over and denounced the attitude of the landowners. The Church hierarchy refused to support the bishop but supported the latifundistas.[69] Bishop Cirarda called for free trade unions and the right to strike, arousing an angry response from Solís. The campaigning Bishops were undeterred. Añoveros supported Cirarda's call by issuing a pastoral letter re-asserting his position. They were supported by the then Bishop of Guadix-Baza Mgr. Gabino Díaz Merchán, who revealed that the braceros still worked for only 100 days a year, suffered from malnutrition, and 41% in the Guadix area lived in caves without electricity or proper sanitation. Cirarda, Añoveros and Díaz Merchán were later to continue their work in Northern Spain, at Santander, Bilbao and Oviedo.

The death of the reactionary Bishop Antonio Pildaín y Zapaín of the Canaries, who had refused permission for the opening of a museum dedicated to the 'heretic' Pérez Galdós, resulted in the appointment of the liberal Mgr. Antonio Infantes Florido. The new Bishop immediately issued a pastoral supporting the Andalusian Bishops' call for more social justice. This is a typical illustration of how the Spanish Church was evolving — an old civil war Bishop died, and was replaced by a 'conciliar' Bishop in spite of Franco's continued right of patronage.

In Cataluña, the death of Modrego Casaus caused a crisis when Franco resorted to his old stratagem of appointing a Castilian to the see — now an Archbishopric. Mgr. Marcelo González Martín, formerly bishop of Astorga, was moved to the Catalan capital where he was received by mass demonstrations demanding the appointment of a Catalan. On 14 May 1968 the Archbishop's throne was burnt by Catalanists. González Martín attempted to meet demands by ensuring the appointment of Catalan auxiliaries. However, the appointment of Castilian Bishops to dioceses in other regions was now becoming unproductive.

A further bone of contention was the position regarding the presence in the Cortes of four bishops, appointed by Franco himself. The four appointees in the 1967 Cortes were all reactionaries and supporters of the close link with the State — Archbishop Morcillo and his even more conservative auxiliary Bishop José Guerra y Campos, Archbishop Pedro Cantero Cuadrado, ex-editor of *Ya* during the period when Catholic Action was a bulwark of the regime, and Bishop Almarcha of León. Demands came from the liberal wing that the bishops renounce this link with Francoism. Morcillo and Guerra felt obliged to defend in public their acceptance of the posts of 'procurador'. Morcillo typifies the dilemma of the ambitious prelate who would previously have climbed the hierarchical ladder by assuring the Holy See of the purity of his conservative credentials. Now he could see a change taking place. He decided to resign from the Cortes in 1969, but he never became a Cardinal. The debate concerning the Church-State relationship continued.

In 1968 Bishop Gúrpide Beope died and a vacancy arose in the see of Bilbao. Such was the state of flux that since 1966 no Bishops had been appointed, and nine sees were vacant. Franco could prevaricate no longer. He had to agree to the appointment of the liberals Infantes (Canaries) Tabera y Araoz (Pamplona) and Cirarda (Santander). With regard to Bilbao an explosive situation was evident. As Franco hesitated the Vatican stepped in. Under the Concordat Franco had no say in the appointment of auxiliaries or apostolic administrators. The Pope appointed Cirarda to supervise the diocese of Bilbao as apostolic adminstrator — a move of great significance in view of Cirarda's liberal record.

In 1968 Cardinal Plá also died and a new primate was needed. Franco would doubtless have liked Cardinal Quiroga or Archbishop Cantero but they were clearly unacceptable after Vatican II. Cardinal Bueno y Monreal was another obvious candidate, but this veteran had always been an independent thinker and earlier in the year had declared himself against Franco's right to appoint Bishops. Finally a compromise candidate arose — Mgr. Vicente Enrique y Tarancón, Archbishop of Oviedo, a learned theologian who had produced many books including several on ecumenism, and three written in quick succession on Vatican II, including *La iglesia del Posconcilio* (1967). He was obviously in the new 'liberal' mould, but had refrained from attacking the regime. Franco accepted him, and he became Primate and Archbishop of Toledo in February 1969. Thirty years previously the incumbent had been Cardinal Gomá y Tomás. The Spanish Church had been transformed and time was running out for Franco's national-Catholicism.

THE CURRENT CRISIS

THE RIFT WIDENS

On 24 January 1969 a state of emergency was declared throughout Spain, brought about largely by industrial unrest and the constant state of siege existing at the universities of Madrid and Barcelona. Archbishop Morcillo and Auxiliary Bishop Guerra y Campos issued a statement approving the wisdom of the government's action. One month later Morcillo was elected president of the Conference of Bishops, defeating the new Primate Mgr. Enrique y Tarancón. The Bishops had affirmed their support for Franco, and shown that the liberals were still in a minority. However, the liberals made up in fervour what they lacked in numbers, and were supported by the Vatican – an unprecedented situation. The Pope expressed his 'anxiety' regarding the position in Spain in June 1969, the first public papal statement on Spain since 'Con inmenso gozo'. The Ministry of Justice responded by deploring the political activities of a minority of prelates.

The balance in the Bishops Conference was changing rapidly. The liberals were gaining ground fast. The XI Bishops Conference of December 1969 saw the conservatives giving ground on the question of Franco's right to episcopal nominations and allowed the conference to express its hostility to the new Ley Sindical. The conservatives leadership was in a state of crisis. Morcillo, forced to resign from the Cortes (rewarded by Franco with the Gran Cruz de Carlos III) still fulminated against progressivism – defending *Humanae Vitae*, attacking the Dutch advocates of married clergy and preventing an international group of liberal clergy from assembling in Madrid.[70]

Morcillo was ill and this led the conservative faction to look more and more to Guerra y Campos for leadership – a mere auxiliary, although a Franco nominee in the Cortes. In June 1971 Morcillo died, and another crisis was unavoidable.

OPUS ZENITH AND DECLINE

Meanwhile Opus Dei remained dominant in government, and enjoyed enormous power in neocapitalism which was now the economic basis of the regime.[71] The two Development Plans had had mixed success, but the tourist boom and the enormous increase in foreign investment had greatly enhanced income per capita.

The October 1969 government saw the Opus grip firmer than ever, but the Matesa financial scandal had shaken those Spaniards who had believed that in spite of their other drawbacks the Opusdeistas were at least honest. Now even that quality was called into question. The Opus had reached the top of the tree. Only descent was possible now. The estrangement of Francoism and the Catholic Church also contributed. Religion was less valid as a legitimizing force than ever before. The Falangist enemies of the Opus hoped for a revival, and an atmosphere of extreme rightist anticlericalism developed. Publications such as *Fuerza Nueva*, *¿Que Pasa?* (which staged a successful campaign

to restore the public Mass for the soul of Hitler[72]) *El Cruzado Español*,
etc., increased circulation and the Opus press was severely hit by the
sanctions against its dailies *Madrid* — which was closed down by the
government, Calvo Serer being forced into exile — and *El Alcázar* which
the Opus were obliged to surrender to its original Falangist owners. In
1973 the Opus myth was exploded. The ruling groups in Spain were
forced to look elsewhere for their ideological prop. For the first time
since 1939 none appeared to be at hand.

THE MOVEMENT FOR DISESTABLISHMENT

It was inevitable that the liberal faction among the hierarchy,
supported by now what would appear to be a majority of the clergy,
would direct their attention towards the problem of the 'confession-
ality' of the Spanish State as affirmed in the 1945 *Fuero de los Españoles*
and re-stated in the 1953 Concordat. What was once the pride and joy
of the Spanish Church and regime was now a source of irritation and
sometimes open conflict. Franco's End-of-Year message in 1969
stated 'la confesionalidad tradicional del Estado . . . corresponde a las
convicciones más profundas de la inmensa mayoría del pueblo español'.
Few were convinced. Just over a year later *Vida Nueva* were to publish
a survey which found that only 5% of Spaniards wished the status quo
to continue and 61% wished the end of the Concordat and separation
of Church and State, and 31% wished to see it drastically revised.[78] The
Bishops discussed the renewal of the Concordat and overwhelmingly
voted, by 60 votes to 10 against a move that the 1953 Concordat be
merely revised. This triumph for the liberals, and the amazingly small
vote in favour of renewing the Concordat is partially explained by the
absence of no less than 30 conservatives who were unable to attend,
largely because of their age. The 'iglesia de la cruzada' was being
changed by natural wastage.

The position of the remaining three Bishops in Cortes remained a
subject of argument. Cantero defended his position, expressing his
loyalty and gratitude to Franco, but the younger clergy demanded their
withdrawal, and renunciation of all clerical rights under the Concordat
as part of a process of disestablishment. Their lack of satisfaction with
the new *Ley de Libertad Religiosa* was also evident. This freedom, held
to be mortal sin until comparatively recently, was now accepted as
inevitable even by the extreme right of the hierarchy, such as Quiroga
Palacios and Cantero Cuadrado.[74] However, the law, when it came, was
a grave disappointment to all advocates of more toleration. It obliged

protestant churches to register with the local municipality, and was boycotted by the majority of Protestant leaders, such as Pastor José Cardona. The local authority registers would contain the names of Protestants permanently on file. The law was greeted as a triumph of the spirit of Vatican II by Blas Piñar – a fact which speaks for itself.[75]

The Jesuits were now largely allied with the progressives. The General Superior Father Arrupe was much given to contradictory and ambiguous speeches, but the younger members of the order were often among the leaders of the movement of renovation within the Spanish church. They opened *Institutos de Teología para Seglares* and their press – *Hechos y Dichos, Razón y Fé*, etc. – were pressurized by the regime. Their proverbial bad relations with Opus Dei contributed. They had lost their grip on the ruling elite and were moving to the opposition, taking many of the former Catholic Action militants with them. A Jesuit, Fr. Bolado, was beaten up by rightist extremists following a demonstration in Barcelona cathedral. These outrages – which under Clause 2343 of Canon Law render the assailants immediately excommunicate – were to increase greatly, often apparently with police connivance. The most flamboyant figure among the Jesuits was Fr. José Díez Alegría, whose brothers, Luis and Manuel, were head of the Civil Guard and Chief of the General Staff of the Army. Fr. Díez Alegría published a book *Creencia y Esperanza* which summarized the liberal position, attacking Church wealth and celibacy and advocating a dialogue with Marxism. Fr. Arrupe instructed that the book be rewritten but Fr. Díez-Alegría refused. He was exclaustrated from the Jesuit order and sent to do pastoral work among the Madrid working class at Vallecas. What the conservatives hoped to gain from this is a mystery.

Another significant gesture made at this time by the liberals was the award by Pax Christi, an organization of Catholic pacifism, of its Pope John XXIII memorial prize to the socialist Archbishop of Recife, Brazil, Dom Helder Câmara, who was the idol of many of the younger clergy. Pax Christi followed this up in 1971 by awarding the prize to José Luis Beunza, the first Catholic to be jailed in Spain for conscientious objection to military service. *Ecclesia* praised the award and defended the rights of conscientious objectors, quoting Paragraph 79 of the Vatican II Pastoral Constitution on the Church in the Modern World.

Priests were becoming increasingly under attack – often physical – from the Guerilleros de Cristo Rey, a right wing neonazi group of thugs and agents provocateurs strongly reminiscent of the similar group depicted in Costa-Gavras' film 'Z' (1968). Blas Piñar lamented 'la pérdida de los valores católicos tradicionales' in the pages of *Fuerza Nueva*.

In the North the involvement of priests in Basque nationalism was very evident. On 16 May 1970 187 priests were in jail — 'abandoned by our Bishops' they said, an allusion to Cirarda's attempts to act as mediator with the regime. This inspired the Bishop to act. He attacked the government for violating the Concordat in arresting priests — often on Church property — and refused to allow the traditional Te Deum for the 'liberation of Bilbao'. In the south a new voice was added to the liberals when Archbishop Benavent Esquín of Granada issued a pastoral denouncing police brutality which had resulted in three deaths during the strike in that city. Sanctuary was offered to strikers in Granada cathedral.

The State of Emergency brought protests from Cirarda, Añoveros and Bishop Jubany Arnau of Gerona, and during the Burgos Trials of 1970 Cirarda and Bishop Argaya Goicoechea of San Sebastian issued a joint pastoral denouncing the procedure of the trial. Bitter exchanges followed with the Ministry of Justice, and *Pueblo* attacked the Bishops for interference in political affairs. Clearly such interference was welcome only when it was in support of the regime.

THE VATICAN ABANDONS FRANCO

The death of Archbishop Morcillo presented the regime with a problem similar to that caused by the death of Cardinal Plá y Deniel three years earlier. As in the case of Bishop Cirarda's appointment to supervise the diocese of Bilbao on the death of Bishop Gúrpide, the Vatican stepped in quickly and appointed an Apostolic Administrator in accordance with the terms of the Concordat which gave Franco no say in these temporary appointments. The administrator appointed was no less a person than the Primate himself, Cardinal Enrique y Tarancón. The Vatican clearly realized that the true seat of power was now the diocese of Madrid—Alcalá rather than the Primacy itself. The clerical *Ya* stated that this was clearly a challenge by the Vatican to Franco, and a clear indication that Rome was embarrassed by the continuation of the Caudillo's right of patronage.

Enrique y Tarancón was hardly a controversial figure like Añoveros or even Cirarda, but he was soon to reveal himself as the Vatican's 'man' and opposed to further links with the Spanish State. On 13 September 1971 he inaugurated the first *Asemblea Conjunta de Obispos y Sacerdotes* — a type of assembly now accepted by the post-conciliar Church, but previously forbidden, notably by Pius X in *Pascendi Gregis* Section III Clause 5. The assembly voted by 170 votes to 56 opposing the Bishops seats in Cortes. Bishop Guerra y Campos and other reactionaries were forced to issue a minority declaration. But the real sensation was yet to come. A resolution was debated, containing the words 'Reconocemos humildemente y pedimos por ello perdón, por no haber sabido ser, cuando fue necesario, verdaderos ministros de la reconciliación', alluding to the Civil War, and clearly rejecting definitively the role of the Church as champion of the 'Cruzada'. That such a resolution was put is important enough, but what really shook the regime was the result of the vote − 137 for, 78 against, with 29 abstentions. A two-thirds majority was required for policy decisions, and this was not obtained, but there was a clear overall majority in favour. In fact the Basque and Catalan clergy were not represented at the assembly. If they had been, the two-thirds would have been obtained easily. As it was, things were bad enough for the regime. The Francoist press raised an outcry and the Guerilleros de Cristo Rey went on the rampage. The notorious vandalism at the Theo gallery, where Picasso canvases were destroyed, occurred on 25 October, priests were attacked and Franco, turning back to his old Falangist faithfuls in November, addressed a congress of the Movimiento warning the Church that to repudiate its past support of the Crusade was to endanger the peace of the nation.

However, Franco clearly wished to avoid an open confrontation with Rome. He allowed the Holy See a free rein in the new list of appointments of December 1971. Cardinal Enrique was confirmed now at Madrid-Alcalá, and the Primacy went to González Martín, relieved no doubt to be back in Castile after his rough ride in Barcelona. The Barcelona see went to Jubany Arnau of Gerona, whose attitude seemed to be moving more and more away from the regime. Cirarda moved south again to Córdoba, and Añoveros replaced him at Bilbao, another blow for the regime, and an appointment which would soon find the bishop on the front pages of the world's press.

The Vatican issued its rewards for service in the form of Cardinal's hats. All were given to liberals, including Archbishop Tabera y Araoz of Pamplona in 1969, but significantly not the prestigious Francoist Cantero − and later Archbishop Jubany, who was soon to become the first Cardinal to speak openly against the regime when he criticized police brutality in Barcelona by speaking of the 'institutionalized violence' of the regime,[76] a statement disavowed by the diplomatic Cardinal Enrique y Tarancón.

The Vatican were also responsible for the setting up of a Justitia et Pax commission to look into social conditions. At its head was another progressive, Bishop González Moralejo of Huelva, an old supporter of Añoveros and Díaz Merchán in their fight for better conditions for Andalusian labourers. A report of the Commission lamented the Church's role in the Civil War and called on Spaniards to fight an unjust system. Economic development was no substitute for justice, the report stated.[77]

The reactionary element appeared confounded. A meeting of pro-Franco clergy (Hermandad Sacerdotal Española) in Archbishop Cantero's diocese of Zaragoza was declared 'unofficial' by the Conference of Bishops. No Cardinal attended, no representative from the Curia was present, and the Papal blessing was withheld.

The repercussions were still resounding from the sensational vote at the assembly of Bishops and priests. Bishop Guerra and the Francoists were forced to seek help abroad. A letter was leaked by the Opus Dei Europa Press organization purporting to have the support of the Pope. It came from the American Cardinal Wright, one of the reactionaries on the Curia, and Prefect of the Congregation of Clergy. It attacked the 'erroneous' position of the Spanish Bishops on theology, and also criticized their involvement in politics. Bishop Guerra welcomed the letter, and affirmed that it had Papal authority. A furious Cardinal Enrique wrote to the Pope for clarification, virtually accusing Guerra of lying. The Cardinal visited Rome shortly after and obtained a public statement from the Secretary of State Cardinal Villot that the views expressed in Cardinal Wright's letter were not shared by His Holiness. The exultant Spanish liberals publicly demanded Wright's dismissal, and Guerra y Campos was removed as Secretary of the Bishops' Conference and replaced by Mgr. Elías Yanes Alvarez, Auxiliary of Oviedo under Díaz Merchán, a champion of the Asturian miners, who freely allowed persecuted strikers asylum in Churches. Guerra y Campos was publicly humiliated and also removed as auxiliary at Madrid for a short while before his appointment as Bishop to the wilds of Cuenca.

Vatican support for the Spanish left was now overt. The Nuncio, Mgr. Dadaglio was asked for asylum by 111 priests and workers pursued by police following a pro-ETA demonstration in Bilbao. The Nuncio agreed and the Spanish government demanded his recall to Rome. The Pope refused. Relations were bad with Franco, and cancellation of the Concordat appeared inevitable.

CHURCH AND STATE TODAY

A statement of the hierarchy regarding Church-State relations was promised at the Bishops' Conference of 2 December 1972. Its publication was delayed for nearly two months. A committee had been set up to prepare the texts. Prominent on the Committee were Archbishop Díaz Merchán, and Bishops González Moralejo, Cirarda and Yanes. The text finally appeared, the voting being 59 in favour, 20 against and 4 abstentions — a clear two-thirds majority. It declared the intention of the episcopacy to renounce all its privileges, to urge withdrawal from the Cortes of Bishops, to reserve the right to speak on social and political matters, and declared the Church's support for political pluralism; after expressing gratitude to the regime for the years of the Concordat, it stated that the time had come for its revision. A worried Archbishop Cantero Cuadrado, friend of Franco, Procurador en Cortes and member of the Consejo del Reino hurriedly visited Rome to discuss the statement. On his return he would offer no comment.[78]

Bishops continued to attract publicity, particularly in the Basque country. The businessman Felipe Huarte was kidnapped by the ETA, and his brother attacked Bishop Javier Oses of Huesca, accusing him of 'Marxism'. The Bishop replied by quoting St. Ambrose — an older authority, he said, than Marx: 'The poor exist because others exist at their expense. What you give as alms to the poor is not yours to give, because it belongs to them since you have taken for yourself what God designed for all.'[79] On 14 April 1973 Fr. Román Landera was beaten up by police in Portugalete following a demonstration after a Mass in which Guerrilleros de Cristo Rey interrupted a sermon. The three policemen had been discovered at the service using a tape recorder 'by order of the civil authorities'. In an unprecedented act, Bishop Añoveros held a solemn ceremony of excommunication of the policemen who attacked Fr. Landera. Similar scenes followed in Madrid, where six priests were beaten, including HOAC counsellor Fr. Eliseo Ruíz de Cortazar. The culmination was the mass rightist anticlerical demonstration following the murder by leftists in Madrid of the secret policeman José Fernández Gutiérrez on May day 1973. The demonstrators demanded 'death to the red Bishops' and 'Tarancon to the firing-squad'. The government was drastically purged of Opus members, although the Opus were largely opposed to the liberals of the hierarchy. Clearly the religious, or religiose, image was no longer regarded favourably by the Francoists. In October 1973 Vatican Secretary of State Mgr. Agustino Casaroli arrived in Madrid for preliminary discussions regarding revision of the Concordat.[80]

The murder of Carrero Blanco halted the advance of liberal Catholicism. A lower key was now inevitable. Franco and Cardinal Enrique embraced publicly, and the new Prime Minister Arias Navarro, after speaking of the 'undeniable conflict of recent years' spoke of a new understanding, though he again warned the Church against inter-ference in the realm of secular politics.[81] It seemed as though a truce was about to be called.

Then, to the dismay of the regime, another 'cause célèbre' exploded. Bishop Antonio Añoveros issued a pastoral on 24 February 1974 in favour of cultural rights for the Basques. It was less anti-regime than many of the Bishop's statements when at Cádiz, but it came at the wrong time. The bishop was put under house arrest, as was his vicar-general Mgr. Ubieta, who had suffered the same fate in 1969 when working with Bishop Cirarda. The wound, partially sewn up after Carrero's murder, had been burst open again by the incredibly inept actions of the regime. Añoveros was told to pack and leave, but he refused, and threatened excommunication on anyone who forced him. As he had put such a threat into practise before, the authorities were afraid to touch him. Nuncio Mgr. Dadaglio, Cardinal Enrique, Cardinal Primate González Martín, Cardinal Jubany were all involved in frantic discussions regarding some sort of compromise solution.[82] The Bishop and vicar-general went into 'retreat'. He received messages of support from almost all the hierarchy, including the reactionary Arch-bishop Cantero. No doubt this crisis will again be temporarily resolved, but the fundamental chasm between Church and State seems now to be unbridgeable.

CONCLUSION

The significance for the future of a total breakdown of relations, with cancellation of the Concordat, must depend on the extent to which the Church retains influence among the people. It has certainly gained respect from the working class, something which it has hardly enjoyed this century. But Spain is becoming secularized. The involvement of the Church with the regime until recently has only served to intensify the trend. Priestly vocations are at an all-time low — 395 ordinations in 1972 compared with an average of over 1,000 per year before 1962.[83] Spanish priests are traditionally taken from rural areas, and Spain is being rapidly urbanised. What does seem clear is that the regime and ruling groups must secularize too, and with the withdrawal of Catholic 'legitimacy' Francoism has nothing to fall back upon. Clichés regarding 'public order' hardly contribute positively, and Arias Navarro's promised 'participation' must remain mere rhetoric unless political parties are legalized. Appeals to old Falangism are grotesque, especially from a regime which has emasculated the Falange. The Church has been the main facade behind which the regime has hidden. If the sotane disguise is shed, the gold braid and epaullettes are all that remains, and the military dictatorship — which is what the regime has been essentially, in spite of its various masks — is hardly likely to improve its chances of entering the EEC. The new 'civilian' government is hardly likely to convince western democratic opinion unless a real democracy is introduced with free trade unions and political parties, in other words, unless Francoism is dismantled. So it appears that however anachronistic it may seem for the Church to have such an influence in a western 'developed' neocapitalist economy, the Church-State split in Spain may in the long run have a profound effect, and mark one of the most important stages in the downfall of a system that has lasted for thirty-five years.

NOTES

1. The text is to be found complete in J. de Iturralde, El Catolicismo y la Cruzada de Franco, vol II, (Bayonne 1960), 22–6 and elsewhere.

2. Ibid., 61–2.

3. This photograph has been widely reproduced, most recently in G. Jackson, A Concise History of the Spanish Civil War (London 1974), 154.

4. A Bahamonde, Un año con Queipo (Barcelona 1938) (Eng. Trans Memoirs of a Spanish Nationalist (London 1939); A. Ruiz Vilaplana, Burgos Justice (New York 1938), passim.

5. Iturralde, op. cit., 56–61.

6. M. Tuñón de Lara, El Hecho Religioso en Espana (Paris 1968) 134–5; Iturralde, op. cit., 265–6.

7. Ibid., 463–4.

8. Tuñón de Lara, op. cit., 135; Iturralde, op. cit., 464–5.

9. Tuñón de Lara, op. cit., 136.

10. Ibid., 138; H. Thomas, The Spanish Civil War (London 1965) 576n.

11. G. Hills, Spain (London 1970), 176; Tuñón de Lara, op. cit., 120.

12. G. Hills, Franco, the Man and his Nation (London 1967), 304; H. R. Southworth, El Mito de la Cruzada de Franco (Paris 1963), 104–6.

13. G. Lewy, The Catholic Church and Nazi Germany (London 1964), 206.

14. The Daily Herald (13 August 1936).

15. H. R. Southworth, Antifalange (Paris 1967), 107–8.

16. Iturralde, op. cit., 302.

17. Ibid., chapters X, XI, XII, passim; G. Jackson, The Spanish Republic and the Civil War (Princeton 1965), 377–8, etc.

18. Thomas, op. cit., 574–7; H. R. Southworth, El Mito de la Cruzada de Franco, 99–104.

19. K. O. Von Aretin, The Papacy and the Modern World (Eng. Trans. London 1970), 191–2.

20. Tuñón de Lara, op. cit., 121.

21. Iturralde, op. cit., 468–70.

22. Tuñón de Lara, op. cit., 145.

23. J. Georgel, El Franquismo (Paris 1970), 190n, 210; P. Nichols, The Politics of the Vatican (London 1968), 153, 342n.

24. H. Thomas, op. cit., 754.

25. For complete text see J. de Iturralde op. cit., vol. III, 551–3.

26. Ibid., vol. II (Bayonne 1960), 468–70.

27. M. Tuñón de Lara, op. cit., 152.

28. G. Brenan, The Spanish Labyrinth (London 1943), 51–2; B. Welles, Spain, The Gentle Anarchy (London 1965), 152–3.

29. E. J. Hughes, Report from Spain (New York 1947), 54–8.

30. M. Fernández Areal, La Política Católica en España (Barcelona 1970), 125–32.

31. Ibid., 129.

32. Welles, op. cit., 245.

33. Hughes, op. cit., 65.

34. Ibid., 79.

35. The Pope, then Cardinal Pacelli, had been largely responsible for Pius XI's virulently anti-Communist Encyclical *Divini Redemptoris* of 1937, which did much to legitimize Franco's rebellion in Catholic eyes. The Encyclical contained a section on 'Communist horrors in Spain'. Another Encyclical was published at about the same time – *Firmissimam Constantium* – which upheld the right of Catholics to take up arms against hostile governments.

36. M. Gallo, Histoire de l'Espagne Franquiste (Paris 1969), 273.

37. The Cold War saw a resurgence in Falangist celebration of Franco's pro-Axis past. See Gallo, 240–47.

38. Fernández Areal, op. cit., 162.

39. Ibid., 163.

40. Iturralde, op. cit., vol. II, 22–6.

41. Fernández Areal, op. cit., 167.

42. Article 6 of the *Fuero de los Españoles* of 1945 guarantees 'liberty of conscience' to non-Catholic Christians.

43. Fernandez Areal, op. cit., 117.

44. Statements made by Gil Robles and other leaders of Acción Popular during the Republic give evidence that many members of Catholic Action were openly sympathetic to an armed insurrection. See P. Preston, The 'Moderate' Right and the Undermining of the Second Republic in Spain 1931–1933', in *European Studies Review* vol. 3, No. 4, 1973.

45. Welles, op. cit., 148–9.

46. Ibid., 167–8.

47. I. Fernández de Castro, La Iglesia de la Cruzada y sus Supervivencias', in Horizonte Español 1966 (Paris, Ruedo Iberico 1966).

48. Gallo, op. cit., 287; Welles, op. cit., 195; J. Georgel, El Franquismo (Paris 1970), 257.

49. Welles, op. cit., 166.

50. V. R. Pilapil, 'Opus Dei in Spain', in The World Today (May 1971), 213.

51. K. O. von Aretin, The Papacy and the Modern World (Eng. Trans. London 1970), 145–8; J. Ynfante, La Prodigiosa Aventura del Opus Dei (Paris 1970), 22–3.

52. A sober account of the activities of Opus Dei is D. Artigues, El Opus Dei en España (Paris 1971).

53. S. G. Payne, Falange (Stanford 1961), 185, 193; Artigues, op. cit., 44–5.

54. Artigues (79) and Pilapil (215) agree that priests account for only 3% of membership.

55. Ynfante draws up lists of Opus members and sympathisers. It is difficult to take seriously all the names included, such as that of the present Prime Minister Arias Navarro who presided over the removal of Opus Dei men from the government. Among foreign Opus associates he quotes several members of the British Labour Party including Mr. Robert Mellish and Lord Longford.

56. Gallo, op. cit., 367; Georgel, op. cit., 198–9.

57. P. Blanshard, Paul Blanshard on Vatican II (London 1967), 26.

58. G. Hills, Spain (London 1971), 355–7.

59. Blanshard, op. cit., 78.

60. Georgel, op. cit., 222; Tuñón de Lara, op. cit , 171.

61. Welles, op. cit., 166; Hills, op. cit., 345–6.

62. Georgel. op. cit., 209–10.

63. Blanshard, op. cit., chapter 17.

64. See note 33.

65. Georgel, op. cit., 225.

66. Welles, op. cit., 142.

67. *The Tablet* (3 June 1972); On the Catholic Action crisis, see Georgel, op. cit., 222–25; E. Miret Magnalena, 'Panorama Religioso 1968', in España Perspectiva (Madrid 1968).

68. Tuñón de Lara, op. cit., 172–3.

69. Miret Magnalena, op. cit.

70. *The Tablet* (8 August 1970).

71. For Opus economic power see especially Ynfante, op. cit.

72. Georgel, op. cit., 206.

73. *The Tablet* (20 February 1971).

74. On religious freedom see D. Nicholl, 'Religious Liberty in Spain', in *Iberian Studies,* vol. 1, No. 1 (1972).

75. Miret Magnalena, op. cit.

76. *The Economist* (15 December 1973).

77. *The Tablet* (8 January 1972).

78. *Blanco y Negro* (27 January 1973).

79. *The Tablet* (24 February 1973).

80. *The Catholic Herald* (9 November 1973).

81. *ABC* (13 February 1974).

82. *The Guardian* (8 March 1974).

83. *The Tablet* (17 March 1973).

REFERENCES

ARTIGUES, D. El Opus Dei en España (Paris 1971).

BAHAMONDE, A. Un año con Queipo (Barcelona 1938) (Eng. Trans. Memoirs of a Spanish Nationalist (London 1939).

BASSO, L. 'Iglesia, Católicos y Política', in Cuadernos de Ruedo Ibérico, No. 11.

BLANSHARD, P. Paul Blanshard on Vatican II (London 1967).

BRENAN, G. The Spanish Labyrinth (London 1943).

CALVO SERER, R. Franco frente al Rey (Paris 1972).

EBENSTEIN, W. G. Church and State in Franco Spain (Princeton 1960).

FERNÁNDEZ AREAL, M. La Política Católica en España (Barcelona 1970).

FERNÁNDEZ de CASTRO, I. De las Cortes de Cádiz al Plan de Desarrollo (Paris 1967).

FERNÁNDEZ de CASTRO, I. 'La Iglesia de la Cruzada y sus Supervivencias', in Horizonte Español 1966 (Paris, Ruedo Iberico 1966).

GALLO, M. Histoire de l'Espagne Franquiste (Paris 1969).

GEORGEL, J. El Franquismo (Paris 1970).

HILLS, G. Franco, the Man and his Nation (London 1967).

HILLS, G. Spain (London 1971).

HUGHES, E. J. Report from Spain (New York 1947).

de ITURRALDE, J. El Catolicismo y la Cruzada de Franco, 3 vols. (Bayonne 1956, 1960, Toulouse 1965).

JACKSON, G. A Concise History of the Spanish Civil War (London 1974).

JACKSON, G. The Spanish Republic and the Civil War (Princeton 1965).

LEWY, G. The Catholic Church and Nazi Germany (London 1964).

MATTHEWS, H. L. The Yoke and the Arrows (London 1958).

MIRET MAGNALENA, E. 'Panorama Religioso 1968', in España Perspectiva 1968 (Madrid).

MIRET MAGNALENA, E. 'Iglesia 1969', in España Perspectiva 1969 (Madrid).

NICHOLL, D. 'Religious Liberty in Spain', in *Iberian Studies*, vol. 1. No. 1 (1972).

NICHOLS, P. The Politics of the Vatican (London 1968).

PALENZUELA, A. Bishop of Segovia, 'Meditación Urgente sobre la Iglesia en España', in España Perspectiva 1972 (Madrid).

PAYNE, S. G. Franco's Spain (London 1968).

PAYNE, S. G. Falange (Stanford 1961).

PILAPIL, V. R. 'Opus Dei in Spain', in The World Today (May 1971).

PRESTON, P. 'The "Moderate" Right and the Undermining of the Second Republic in Spain 1931–1933', in *European Studies Review* vol. 3, No. 4, 1973.

PRESTON, P. 'General Franco's Rearguard', in *New Society* (29 November 1973).

'P.B.' 'Significación religiosa, económica y política del Opus Dei', in Horizonte Español 1966 (Paris, Ruedo Iberico 1966).

RUIZ VILAPLANA, A. Burgos Justice (New York 1938).

SOUTHWORTH, H. R. Antifalange (Paris 1967).

SOUTHWORTH, H. R. El Mito de la Cruzada de Franco (Paris 1963).

THOMAS, H. The Spanish Civil War (London 1965).

TRYTHALL, J. W. D. Franco (London 1970).

TUNON DE LARA, M. El Hecho Religioso en España (Paris 1968).

VIDAL, JOAN 'Iglesia y Sociedad en España', in Cuadernos Ruedo Ibérico, No. 36.

VON ARETIN, K. O. The Papacy and the Modern World (Eng. Trans. London 1970).

WELLES, B. Spain, the Gentle Anarchy (London 1965).

YNFANTE, J. La Prodigiosa Aventura del Opus Dei (Paris 1970).